LEO SMITH

Leo Smith

A Biographical Sketch by

Pearl McCarthy

UNIVERSITY OF TORONTO PRESS

Preface

Leo Smith hated tombstones. He felt that nature ordered these matters better for the birds, leaving only memory of flight and song when they had gone. Therefore he would not be well served by a biographical sketch written only to memorialize his personal attainments as composer, violoncellist, critic, fellow of the Royal Manchester College of Music, and professor at the University of Toronto.

But his career had more than personal significance. He was a leader in a particular phase of cultural development throughout one of the most formative periods in the country's social history. His work was at maturity between the two World Wars, and for seven creative years thereafter. It thus spanned the years between the old music and the new, between the time when artistic education was private and the time when people fastened their cultural hopes on public education and government funds, between the last days when white gloves and white ties were worn to drawing-room musicales and the days when men without ties might dash to recitals.

This is a period too near to have received the boon of the historian's objective treatment, and yet too antique to come within the focused view of some men to whom the present day is indebted for its cultural vitality. As a result, the foundations of such cultural activities as are found in 1956 are not always clearly descried, and those attempting to sum up the present situation sometimes find perplexing factors left over. Such puzzles are bound to remain so long as it is taken for granted that one period of musical expansion ended with the First World War and that entirely new factors accounted mainly for developments twenty years later. This probably was true only with regard to such things as the devices based on electronic inventions.

In this period of development Leo Smith not only composed and performed for the public but carried his public with him into the new era. He was one of the most picturesque and often idolized artists on the Canadian scene. To crowds at large popular concerts such as the Toronto Proms, he represented the music maker, although he might be at the time only one man in an organization that filled a stage, seeming to strive for anonymity as he kept his poetic head bent over his instrument. His own history, then, is also history of an interesting and changing musical scene and valuable for its intimate connection with it.

Leo Smith himself suggested one of the themes of a sketch such as this when he wrote in the *Conservatory Quarterly Review*: "While I wish to pipe Canadian tunes, readers of this Quarterly will observe what I fear will always be: that they are sung to an English ground bass." For that reason something of his early years in England has been related here. He helped to prepare ground in Canada on which creative work could grow as an indigenous rather than an exotic transplant, but his own contribution was based on a synthesis of values found in the Old World and the New.

He left no diaries, no list of accomplishments. Sometimes, relaxing beside his fire, he would let slip a veiled reference. Then the intimate friend might know that the person Leo Smith did not name was Strauss or Elgar, or an ancestor at the court of the first Elizabeth, or Mme Patti. They were wraiths slipping across the back of the stage in luminous shadow, and he would not bring them forward. Some light has been turned on that background now for the sake of showing how and where Leo Smith formed his tastes and his standards.

He did leave the testament of his compositions (some published, some of the best unpublished), his critical commentaries, and the friendships which, with him, were also a gentle art. All have contributed to this account of their creator. It has been thought unfitting, in the modest scope of a sketch, to proffer footnotes. Some further indication of the sources of material used should, however, be given. These have been the personal papers of Leo Smith; music and literary publications by him; unpublished manuscripts, musical and literary; newspaper reviews, Birmingham, Manchester, Toronto, New York; standard works of reference in music (dates have been checked by reference to the private papers of L.S.); information supplied by Miss Marie Smith of Birmingham, England; the author's personal experience of the period covered and of what Leo Smith said and did.

The late Mrs. Leo Smith made possible this memoir of her husband. She was most grateful, as am I, to the artists who have collaborated: Dora de Pedery Hunt whose portrait study forms the frontispiece, and Richard Brown, who has drawn the chapter decorations. I am indebted to Helena McCarthy McMillan for practical assistance; to Marion Brown, who first suggested the writing of this sketch and who helped collect the music. A writer may well appreciate the judgment and kindness of those who represent the University of Toronto Press.

P. McC.

Toronto, March 1956

Contents

ix

LEO SMITH

1. *An English Ground Bass*

Birmingham Town Hall was crowded one night in 1889 for a performance in the Harrison concert series. It was known that a new 'cellist was to be presented, a prodigy who had already surprised audiences and was now to give a major programme. Only those in the front rows could see the small performer and as the recital got under way, listeners began to stand up, blocking each other's view. Mr. Harrison took a rug from the floor, threw it over the grand piano and lifted the performer, his small chair, and his large instrument on top of the piano to finish the recital.

This was the professional début at the age of eight of Joseph Leopold Smith who, known as Leo Smith, spent his youth in England and his maturity in Canada. He was born in Birmingham in 1881 and died in Toronto in 1952.

That night in Birmingham Town Hall, with the child holding an audience from his perch on the grand piano, interest was increased by local pride that the prodigy was a native of the city. The Smiths then lived in a large Victorian house in Monument Road. In the audience there happened to be Dr. Gibbs Blake, physician to Mme Patti. He told Mme Patti of Leo Smith; she later saw and heard him, and offered to adopt him, promising to arrange for the best tutors to travel with him. Mme Patti's suggestions usually were carried out—from her first conquest of recital audiences to the time when graves were moved so that she could be buried in Paris on a main path of Père Lachaise cemetery. But not this time. Her kindness was appreciated; but the child's parents felt that a regular academic education was better than private tutoring in an atmosphere of fame and virtuosity. The Gibbs Blakes and the child's 'cello teacher, W. H. Priestley, agreed with the parents.

But, as the family had more breeding than money, some method of ensuring the boy's advanced studies seemed wise. Frank Earle Huxley, Mrs. Gibbs Blake's son by a former marriage, and Carl Fuchs, the 'cellist, became joint guardians for the boy's musical education. A lifelong friendship grew up between Fuchs and Leo Smith, and the older musician wrote a reminiscent review in the *Manchester Evening News* when Leo Smith's music was included in an Empire broadcast of Canadian works by BBC in 1935. Through Carl Fuchs the boy came to know and play chamber music with leading musicians including composers.

The other side of the guardianship provided experiences that had an essential effect on his later art. The Gibbs Blakes lived in Worcestershire near Birmingham in a house of the country mansion type, and Leo Smith spent much time there. They showed themselves ideal guardians for sensitive genius by their first gift—a pony and gig. Mr. Huxley enjoyed driving with the child, sometimes for days, sauntering through lanes, valleys, villages. The children of the Smith family had known the large houses of some relatives and family connections, but the pony-and-gig days at the Gibbs Blakes' were particularly powerful in confirming a special sensitivity to nature that distinguished Leo Smith from childhood to his death.

In some of the most beguiling humour of modern fiction, Virginia Woolf has described this state of mind. Orlando, it will be remembered, had been able to change from an English ambassador to a southern gypsy, dropping completely all physical and spiritual attributes of his former English self—except his attitude to nature. The gypsies actually found Orlando gazing at a field where there was nothing at which to look. They realized that Orlando felt part of this thing, nature, and would never be quite one of them.

Less percipient than the gypsies, some men who recognize the elemental in the beat of the savage tom-tom, forget to look for it in the cultivated art of the composer Leo Smith. His feeling for nature did not dominate, but in a definite way did complement what might be called his spiritual life. He was neither an animist nor a mere outdoor man, although he did enjoy outdoor sports and played fast badminton and tennis until past sixty, when he had trouble with his eyes. Beautiful landscapes and peaceful skies offered their accrued dividends; but it was a deeper appreciation of the elements which drew him out to walk through blinding wind and sleet. He was homing to the sources of art as well as life. He had an aptitude for feeling what scientists have been at pains to impress on the public (and sometimes on their confrères)—that man is part of the earth and the cosmos. When the pony-and-gig days were recalled decades later beside a mid-winter Canadian fireplace, Leo Smith's countenance would take on a blissful, far-away dreaminess that caused one to remember Orlando. Orlando could not explain his attitude to the gypsies; Leo Smith could not explain his to more than a few performers of his music.

While the poetic results of this early effect of nature appeared in his compositions, curious practical results came also. As an Englishman new to canoeing, he astonished people on a river in Western Canada by his ability to paddle up a swift current. Most people paddle *against* a current. Leo Smith, with his aptitude for co-operating with nature, discovered how to utilize the anomalies in the current to assist in propelling his craft— a principle well known to educated engineer-designers and primitive Indians.

Several of his traits were inborn. On the maternal side he was a Turnour, direct descendant of the Turnour who was Lord Chief Baron of the Exchequer at the court of

Charles I, and of Turnours who had been landed digni-taries since the time of Henry IV. Through his mother, Amy, and his grandfather, Michael, he was the great-grandson of the first Lord Winterton. From this side he fell heir to musical talent. His mother was a pianist who had studied at the Royal Academy, who was described as having genius, and who never dropped her career although she had seven children.

His paternal stock was yeoman rather than aristocratic but equally interesting, and purebred English. His father, William Smith, was a descendant of the Blood family of Stratford-on-Avon whose home was Shakespeare's birth-place. They were the last private residents of the house, and, when it became a national trust, a great-great aunt of Leo Smith's, a Mrs. Willey, remained as the first custodian. William Smith, obtaining his education largely by his own efforts, became a French master teaching in a Birmingham grammar school.

The home this pair founded gave the seven children bountiful culture plus shortage of cash—and ineradicable standards of independence. The only strain was some in-compatibility between the parents. It is mentioned here because Leo Smith's reactions to it were relevant to certain views on art which he held all his life. It has been learned since his death from one of the family that the children while still young agreed among themselves not to mention this unhappiness even to each other. They never broke the rule.

In later life, Leo Smith frequently discussed with the present writer a relevant principle embodied in his music.

He held firmly that pain and discord were not creative, that to seek a non-creative effect in a work that purported to be creative was an anomaly. He was an irreconcilable foe of what used to be called the ash-can school, contending that this was not realism but a weak escape from the realism of the sometimes arduous path to beauty. It is a much-debated question, and all that is required here is recognition that Leo Smith's style was based on convictions, that those convictions had been present since childhood and long before he had read Mozart's famous dictum on never expressing a painful experience in a way to give pain.

The children of this home became individuals talented in the humanities. There was Arnold Smith, authority on Browning, writer on English usage, and poet; some of his poems Leo Smith set to music. There is the brilliant sister who became a Roman Catholic, and after being a nun for years, was released from her vows and returned to secular life as a scholarly teacher. There is the sister who, maintaining the Stratford-on-Avon tradition, became an outstanding Shakespearean librarian. Each has shown courageous attachment to convictions. Literary and musical interests are found in constant cross-reference throughout their work. In religion, the family came within the broad Anglican span and read Swedenborg.

Leo Smith began his education at private schools and at the Birmingham Midland Institute of Music. Later he went to the Royal Manchester College of Music where he graduated with record marks in harmony and composition, and took his Mus.Bac. from Manchester University. In

1925 the Royal Manchester College of Music recognized him as a distinguished alumnus by making him an honorary fellow.

Some of his early dates vary casually even in biographical notes which he himself supplied for standard reference works. Probably this variation was due partly to his own indifference to such matters, and partly to his enchanting handwriting. It had calligraphic charm but formed a major enigma for typesetters, and he never used a typewriter.

What is known certainly is that he played in major orchestras in his 'teens. Carl Fuchs recorded that he had sent Leo Smith as a small boy to the ensemble group of the Royal Manchester College of Music and that Dr. Brodsky had said to Fuchs after the first rehearsal: "Well, you have sent me a perfect musician."

He became a member of the Hallé Orchestra and later went up to London to the Covent Garden orchestra, on the personal invitation of Hans Richter. While in Manchester he taught 'cello and theory and filled many playing engagements. His ensemble work of the time connects his name with that interesting old institution, the Gentleman's Concert Hall, because it was for a performance there of Spohr's Double Quartet that the young 'cellist was chosen as one of the second group to play with the Brodsky Quartet.

He found time for considerable composition. There is a Manchester review of a Symphonic Movement in E Minor, but this is not now among his papers. The *Manchester City News* reviewed performances of songs in manuscript by Leo Smith to lines by Shelley, Leigh Hunt, Blake and Poe.

One of these, "Oranges," appears on an early programme by John Coates in Bechstein Hall. Reviewers already spoke of his "scholarly interpretation," his "impressionism," and the "modernism" of his writing.

From the English orchestral years came the recollections of composers and conductors. (He was scrupulous about crediting quotations or borrowed ideas, and all recollections not so credited in his writings were his own.) Leo Smith heard Richter say: "Mozart is a young man with a bright future"; and heard, with less approval, Richter's comment that he didn't play French music because there wasn't any. He recalled that when Delius took the baton, "the stick trembled like an aspen leaf." He recollected from chamber music evenings with Elgar and with Elman, that Elman became the pure artist in chamber music, dropping his stage style entirely. He found Bartok's personality shy, "contrasting with the strength of his music." He saw that, during rehearsals of *Pelléas et Mélisande*, Debussy refused to say anything, holding that the music must speak for itself. He developed great sympathy with conductors trying to give effective concert performances of Wagner with a solo singer, for he watched Richter try several expedients including having the singer on a raised dais so that, without his reducing the orchestral volume to un-Wagnerian intent as mere accompaniment, the vocal timbre might carry through.

Not all his time was spent in such pursuits, however. Travel and excursions varied his days. He frequently holidayed in Switzerland with Mr. Huxley, and he made numerous and apparently fairly hilarious trips to Continental festivals with young musicians. He particularly enjoyed one "with a posse of 'cellists" to Bayreuth where, owing to shortage of accommodation in the town, one section of the party was quartered with the police, the other in the lunatic asylum.

He learned to be a trouper. He was one of the Forty Thieves, as members of the touring nucleus of the Hallé Orchestra were called because they were the lucky ones who got paid for more performances. A good player might pick up as many as thirty *Messiah* engagements at Christmas time. "There was the element of monotony in playing the same work so many times," Leo Smith recalled; "but then one got to know it very well and there were interesting experiments in the art of playing and sleeping at the same time, and so one passed a very pleasant evening."

The "very pleasant evening" epitomized the attitude he took to the exigencies of trouping. The best proof of how solid his trouping and theatrical experience had been was given decades later in Canada. During the first visit to Toronto by the Sadler's Wells Ballet, a 'cellist was suddenly taken ill and somebody suggested that the only man who might play ballet music (including Benjamin Britten's) without rehearsal was a Professor Smith of the University of Toronto. Leo Smith agreed to go down. Then the hearts of the conductor and the players sank. Into the orchestra pit came a frail, greying scholar, feeling his way carefully because he had had an eye operation recently, and looking anyway as if he would not be at home in an atmosphere less withdrawn than Erasmus' study. But it was curtain time and they had to begin. Leo Smith's bowing arm began to create rhythm from the shoulder blade. A ballet score, in which the music seems to have had everything done to it in somebody else's indecipherable handwriting, was a familiar sight to him from old days. He was smiling in the old game of keeping one eye on the music, one on the conductor, and somehow half an eye and ear on the dancer's mood. At the intermission, the conductor reached him first and threw his arms around him. Players, prima ballerina, and ballerinas not prima followed, with kisses. The professionals knew he had performed a remarkable feat. They found him gallant and gay. Then, like one of ballet's own characters who may dance in the night but must fade before dawn, the youthful trouper slipped away, and the aging professor went back to his study, put on his green eye-shade, and faced his last works and his ever-increasing pain. It had been a few hours stolen from time, recaptured from his English youth prior to 1910.

In 1910, favoured, successful, and more widely experienced than most musicians, he suddenly decided to come to Canada. He never explained just why, but observation through later years seems to justify offering an explanation. He loved being part of new developments. His manners and his dress were conservative, but he had the spirit of a pioneer to his last days. He could make quick decisions, and he thought little of people who, having made a decision, wavered. The newer world of Canada appealed to him. He sailed and, with two introductory calling cards, paid his respects to Dr. Edward Fisher, principal of the Toronto Conservatory of Music.

2. *Canadian Tune*

The gaslight era of industrial expansion was closing when Leo Smith came to Canada in 1910. The arts still enjoyed the favour and prosperity that came from private patronage and, while that advantage might be limited mainly to the urban few, what there was of it was very real and psychologically comfortable.

One reason for the comfort was the more homogeneous nature of society. A perusal of old faculty lists of the Toronto Conservatory of Music reveals a preponderance of Anglo-Saxon names. Moreover, with some exceptions, both patrons and professionals came from the same social class, the middle one where families found the private means for private education in, and enjoyment of, the arts. There were degrees of affluence, from penury to wealth, but there was similarity in concepts of education and of what made a desirable existence. If the odd Slavic, Latin, Scandinavian, Germanic, or British outsider joined the ranks, he too usually came from a comparable social group and fairly soon felt himself part of the Toronto circle.

The cultural limitations of such a society are easy to see and have been pointed out often. It has less often been noted that the older social ensemble had one advantage: if patrons and professionals had any commerce with each other at all, they stood a sporting chance of understanding each other's aims. To this understanding Leo Smith immediately contributed something more. He was tremendously impressed by the fact that many men not only had made fortunes in the short period after the pioneer opening of the country but also had founded some cultural institutions. And he became Canadian to the core, not surpassed by any musician, Canadian-born or foreign-born, in his appreciation and understanding of earlier pioneers. Although himself a product of Old World culture in a personal as well as a public way, he never thought of himself as a kind of cultural missionary. He was joining the ranks of Canadians to share their labours, their satisfactions or their disappointments. From this beginning, his attitude to the Canadian public grew until it became a distinctive contribution in applied aesthetics. Whatever success or disappointments he knew, he never felt cut off across a gulf from the lay public. He might run into temporary enmity with fellow professionals over policy, but he loved the public. They in turn thought he belonged to them. He was their nightingale.

The more homogeneous and settled nature of society on his arrival facilitated this understanding. The taste of old patrons may seem narrow in comparison with that of today's audiences, who have had a sampling of most everything by radio, television, or records. But they at least were exposed to sufficient musical evidence of one kind to warrant hearty likes and dislikes of their own. Some, as Leo Smith recalled of Dumas, "detested even bad music." Others learned to like good music.

In a day when men did not turn in their tastes as they now turn in their cars for new models, the musician was less likely to find himself on the used-car lot after a brilliant trial run. One concrete example may be given. A business man who had arrived in Toronto quite ignorant in the arts, prospered and subscribed to the big choirs. He grew fond of English choral music. Forty years later, in his last illness, he asked his doctor to let him attend one last performance by the Mendelssohn Choir under Dr. Fricker, to hear Walton's *Belshazzar's Feast*, and he was told that he might go if he kept perfectly still. When at the end, he jumped to his feet waving his hat and cheering, he answered those who expostulated that he might kill himself: "What does it matter! They have done so well." It is probably safe to suppose that today's musicians would be grateful for more patrons, of any kind of taste, who would stay with them forty years and willingly shorten their lives to cheer them at the end. This man was a friend of Leo Smith; his children, heirs to musical advantages their father never had, were among Leo Smith's devoted followers, and typical of others.

Leo Smith's attitude from his first days in Canada bred continuity of interest. In some cases, it eventually meant three generations of music followers, with grandparents, parents, children, all participating in some way. This tendency was put in words during the forties when somebody lamented that certain compositions by Leo Smith had not been published. Betty Bruce Brown, then a young girl, asked her mother: "But can't the music be kept alive if all teach the music to their children?"

Another aspect of his contribution to a sense of community in musical Toronto was determined in his first years in Canada. At a rehearsal of the old Toronto Symphony Orchestra under Frank Welsman, he met a young violinist, Lena Hayes, described in a Conservatory publication of the time as "one of the most successful lady violinists that Canada has produced." She had just returned from graduate studies in England. They fell in love and were married. Leo Smith always liked feminine company and enjoyed the friendship of women; but it was his extraordinary fortune to marry at the outset of his career the only woman he ever loved, the one who never ceased to enchant him as his ideal.

This meant that, especially after the Rosedale house was built at 117 Park Road, "The Leo Smiths' "—garden as well as house—became a Toronto musical centre. It was not, however, a kind of celebrity salon. People who were there had the common bond of sharing Leo Smith's ideals, and a "family" was made of diverse friendships which included the exquisite Rosita Chevalier Boutell de Weissmann of Buenos Aires, whose father had thirty motor cars, and also students who had none; priests who were studying music; journalists and business men; Attila de Pedery, old friend of British Foreign Office men in Budapest; and Canadian-bred musician Hayunga Carman. On one characteristic Sunday afternoon, Leo Smith was wearing the striped-trouser grey-waistcoat attire which was normal for him on Sunday. Percy Grainger, for whom he had much affection, had arrived wearing white ducks, carrying a red silk umbrella, and with his hair like an attractive motif for "Shepherd's Hey," which was normal for him. The two sat together on the piano bench, playing and singing each other's compositions and laughing until the tea wagon made more urgent demands. After her husband's death Lena Hayes Smith kept up the tradition, although on a quieter scale, until shortly before her death in February of this year.

Throughout the years of his life in Canada, Leo Smith continued his career as teacher, performer, and composer in many places and under many auspices. From 1911 he was a member of the staff of the Toronto Conservatory of Music. Its yearbook for that date had advertised that the Conservatory offered students "a thorough artistic and musical education in all branches of the art, preparing them fully for the teaching profession, for concert, church and platform work as well as for the drawing room or the social circle." The closer relation between music and the drawing-room or personal life at that time was epitomized by the principal's studio. The writer remembers it well from a day when she was taken, as a small pudge, to play a piece for Dr. Fisher so that a teacher might be assigned. The parent and the principal bowed and exchanged compliments, but the pudge stood transfixed by the sight of the curtains. It was common enough in Edwardian times to have lace curtains reach the floor or even spread out on it like a court train. But these curtains, by some trick of starching, fell in a cascade on the carpet in a way wonderful to behold. The room had photographs and other items representing the personal life of the owner, as did most studios. It was no office-with-piano. But the Conservatory was not behind in modern amenities. An account of a reception held in the principal's studio in 1908 spoke of the wonderful hues of the ladies' dresses, "satins shimmering under the electric light bulbs."

Frank Welsman was delighted to have in the Toronto Symphony Orchestra the 'cellist who had been so highly valued by Richter. Leo Smith and Frank Welsman became friends, enjoying studying scores together. The 'cellist brought from his English experience an exceptionally wide and firm grounding in orchestral work. He was incapable of losing his place in a score and was sometimes called the "seeing-eye dog" of an orchestra when any section inclined to falter.

He occasionally said, in playing as in teaching, "I can't"; but he meant, for reasons best known to himself, "I won't." He would stop dead if a careless partner toppled a music stand. On the other hand, he would go to any possible lengths in helping conscientious but less experienced players. On one occasion a fine string player had returned to orchestral work after some years in private life, was nervous, and had been humiliated at rehearsal by playing a harmonic off pitch. Before the concert, Leo Smith whispered: "If you think you are going to be nervous, I will hold that C sharp; nobody will notice." Assured that the player felt under control, he contented himself by sweeping this violinist a conspicuous bow. Intonation was perfect.

Leo Smith engaged in chamber music from his arrival. He played with Frank Blachford in the old Toronto String Quartet. Public chamber music was rare then, as it still is, but the last days of the drawing-rooms were enhanced by it. It was fairly common for people who could afford it to give musicales as a form of at-home, sometimes in the great houses which still stood as private residences on Jarvis and Sherbourne as well as in the newer homes of Rosedale. The Toronto String Quartet also played for hosts in Buffalo.

In addition to such at-homes, there were series of drawing-room musicales for which tickets were sold. There is already an archaic flavour in the explanation given at the time that, because of the limited size of these Toronto houses, audiences for such affairs had to be limited to 200. Leo Smith appeared as 'cellist or commentator at a number of these chamber music events, and some of his songs were sung by Mrs. John Macdonald and by Miss Winifred Hicks-Lyne.

Within a few months of Leo Smith's coming to Toronto, his own compositions came into use. The first to present his songs on this side of the Atlantic was Canadian-born

Margaret Huston who, after including them in a Toronto recital in December 1910, sang them in the Belasco Theatre in New York in 1911. By May 4, 1914, the *Toronto World* had a headline: LEO SMITH GAINING WIDE REPUTATION AS COMPOSER AND ARTIST. In 1914, the June issue of *Musical America* reviewed the new Schirmer album of his songs, noting editorially that "he has more acute harmonic sense than have many of those American composers whose works are on the programs of our best singers."

Up to the end of the First World War, we find reference to "British" or "American" composers when men like Leo Smith are mentioned. This was true of Healey Willan as of Leo Smith. But they had learned their trade as composers and had been through the test of audience reception. After the First World War, when they had been writing in the Canadian context, these men appeared as the trail-blazers for the concept of the "Canadian composer." Besides which, a certain young Canadian of genius, Ernest Mac-Millan, who very soon contributed strongly to musical composition in Canada, had been breaking a record by composing the work for his Oxford doctorate in music while interned in Ruhleben Prison Camp in Germany.

Leo Smith's varied activities in teaching, performing, and composing were well established in the Canadian setting when the World War broke out. Because of an internal injury from which he suffered, he was not accepted for military service, and his life for the duration became "carrying on," as it was called. The carrying on told when the musical scene expanded in peace.

In 1918, Dr. A. S. Vogt, who had succeeded as principal

of the Toronto Conservatory on the death of Dr. Fisher, singled out Leo Smith for a literary work that has no exact counterpart in Canadian letters. Dr. Vogt had decided that the Conservatory should publish a quarterly magazine, but of a special sort, differing from those in which the editorial section, if it exists at all, takes a minor place. There were to be articles, but stress was to be laid on the editorial section, and this was not to be merely a succession of musical Judgment Days. It was to form a kind of running commentary on musical life, which would aim to inculcate criteria, and to reflect the attitude of a man of taste.

This was a difficult assignment, but it was one into which Leo Smith could put his heart, since he disliked the didactic attitude anyway and believed that education in its broad sense meant the development of the mind and the heightening of social enjoyment. (He left those views on record when, on behalf of the Proms, he wrote a brief for the Hope Commission on Education, 1950.) He was, moreover, a devoted amateur of the essay and read widely in poetry and the *belles lettres* of prose. Therefore the epicure set to work.

His writing manifested the combination of grace, intellectual courtesy, and musical knowledge which later caused the senior common room of the University of Toronto to regard him as an adornment to academic life as well as a teacher. It glowed with humour, entertained by wittily placed quotations, offered authoritative musical discussions, and (perhaps most important of all) it abounded in comments to suggest principles beneath the passing show.

It may be regretted that Leo Smith, having more literary

gifts than most professional writers, did not take a professional attitude to the essay form until later years. He knew that the essayist who will modulate back perfectly to his tonic key after an excursion of a few hundred words needs a literary technique as facile as Mozart's composition. He saw himself, however, as a professional musician, but as an amateur writer whose very respect for professionalism might make it presumptuous to master form in that field. Thus his early writings were left more like brilliant diaries, and it might not be possible to select for an anthology of essays any single one that would give a just representation of his unusual gift. As a body of writing, however, his editorials in the old *Conservatory Quarterly Review* had distinction and showed his ability to criticize by principles rather than by preferences. Dr. Vogt's idea plus Leo Smith's talent produced that extremely rare thing—a kind of public diary of contemporary taste.

It is conceivable that, in a day when Canada has a larger population and more Foundations to sponsor publications, selections from this editorial diary might be reprinted for their interest as Canadian social history, as they give evidence of attitudes and aspirations for two decades between the First and the Second World Wars. A research student of a future century could visualize causes, events, and results if, by some fantastic chance, he was left only Leo Smith's editorials to contemplate.

He would feel the relief after the Armistice; the enthusiasm for new ideas in the 1920's; the intermittent trade depressions and influenza epidemics; the coming of mass communication by wireless and the fears that listeners would become, musically, the idle rich; the movement to have the arts recognized in academic education; the prospects of state support to take the place of, or to complement, the passing private patronage of musical institutions.

He might infer, in the following years, the more embattled 1930's when men who had fought together to push back cultural frontiers often disagreed on what constituted art in general and music in particular; when discussions of issues became more sinewy; when changing political-social concepts and the grim carnival of the Great Depression complicated liberal progress; and through it all, the vitality of effort as expressed by the pen of a poetic 'cellist writing into the night when he had finished his music for the day.

Topics called to memory at random from the *Conservatory Quarterly Review* may suggest why the editorials seemed like a kind of Anatomy of Pleasure—

The use of the Te Deum in times of national rejoicing. . . . A note that a press-cutting agency has recently written to William Byrd c/o the Aeolian Hall, offering to supply him with clippings; and that the Department of Inland Revenue has sent a tax form to Mr. Gay c/o The Beggar's Opera. . . . Leo Smith's prognostication that a renaissance in English music is very near. . . . A memo that there was a musicians' strike in Rome in the time of Tiberius, and that the government settled it by feasting the musicians and then, when they were drunk, rushing them back to work in chariots. . . . An appraisal of Debussy's contribution to music. . . . A note that, at a recent reception in the Mansion House, the Lord Mayor sang and the Lady Mayoress played two-piano duos with an ex-sheriff. . . . A discussion of Holst and his use of the Augmented Fourth. . . . A reminder that the arts survive turmoil; was not the Paris Conservatoire mooted during the Red Terror of 1794 and founded the year after? . . . A profound appreciation of Elgar. . . . A reminder that, at an early performance of *Sœur Angélique,* the donkey on stage brayed in response to Puccini's donkey motif; Ernest Newman said it was unfair to dismiss the donkey, as it was only exerting the singer's prerogative of showing the composer how to improve.

There was space also for some terse comment on the problems of creating standards in a large country of old and new parts and uneven economic development. In this connection Leo Smith left one of the most poignant human stories for the Canadian record. As examiner for the Toronto Conservatory he had travelled in 1929 to a remote Prairie town on a train that was "like the 5th species of counterpoint—mixed." The weather was bad, but parents had left their farms and struggled in over the roads so that the children might be on time for examinations. The little girls wore their party frocks, and "the graceful thank-you after the ordeal is over would melt the heart of a public prosecutor." But the teacher in their district seemed to have thought that Prelude and Fugue was just a double-barrel name for one item—and the young candidates had prepared only the Prelude.

In the late 1920's Leo Smith was busy with other writing. Earlier he had published a small textbook *Musical Rudiments,* which has been used in practically all English-speaking countries. In 1931 his important book, *Music of the 17th and 18th Centuries* was published. This stands as an admirable answer to the problem of producing an analytical historical volume that any intelligent layman may enjoy, but which gives tersely the information needed by a student not inclined to tackle the reading of a long book. Pleasant style marks the chapters which precede tables of dates, and even specimen examination questions. For years it was prescribed reading at the Toronto Conservatory and is still recommended, although recourse has often to be made to libraries, as most booksellers have no readily available copies.

The cultural scope and the sympathy so patent in Leo Smith's writings show why, as a teacher, he was sought not only by local students but by graduates from other countries. The smooth pace of his chronicles might suggest, to one who did not know the facts, that they were the product of leisured ease. The opposite was the case.

He never inherited money, and he kept his charges moderate, although not entirely from modesty. The too-moderate price of tickets for recitals betokened his own private brand of pride. It is an attitude which crops up now and again among professional people of much talent, including some doctors who feel more dignity in treating patients who have faith in their work but can pay only three dollars, than in attending querulous clients who might not miss three thousand. Leo Smith was no egalitarian and had no dislike of money and fine estate for himself or others, providing these could be got unostentatiously; but he had inherited some standards from the class which used to think ambition undignified. His ideals caused him to give steady application to professional duties. Even his composing was relegated to off hours. He felt that an artist, as much as any other man, should take personal responsibility for his own financial position, and he disliked people who acted on the belief that the world owed them a living.

Persistent work was made possible by a characteristic manifest in his compositions and writings—his capacity for delight. He more than once carried off the prize from a masquerade ball. Gardens, choice company, public speaking, the theatre, travel, land and sea gave him enjoyment. He was curious about anything from hydrodynamics to stock broking and the productions of *Guys and Dolls*. He once asked a younger friend: "Please, dear child, explain to me what you mean by your word 'corny.'" When Hazel Scott played Boogie-Woogie in Toronto, he and she had a happy encounter. Cricket, swans, nursery puddings, good ale, all attracted him.

Over the years, his interest in education was apparent in many ways. His connection with the Toronto Conservatory continued from 1911 until his death in 1952. The Conservatory became a unit within the University of Toronto in 1921, and Leo Smith was appointed as a lecturer at the University in 1927. In 1938, when the University of Toronto established an Arts course in Music, he was made a professor, along with Dr. Healey Willan, with Sir Ernest MacMillan as dean of music. He maintained his professorial duties until retiring in 1950. His direct educational work thus covered more than forty years at the Conservatory and twenty-three years as a faculty member of the University of Toronto.

University life delighted Leo Smith, and he particularly enjoyed playing at Hart House and having his works presented there. The Hart House connection accounted for some of his most unusual productions because the Hart House chest of viols was made available to the Conservatory String Quartet when he was its 'cellist, and later to him personally. There are definite rules regarding the use of these Hart House viols: "The instruments are museum pieces and should be treated as such; at the same time they are not merely objets d'art and they should be available for use under certain conditions. . . . The viols are to be used only by experienced string musicians for rendering music appropriate to them."

"Music appropriate to them" meant that Leo Smith was invaluable in his ability to realize, for various groups of viols, old and sometimes fragmentary literature of their period. In their physical care, he was expert. If he had to take home the Hart House viola da gamba at night, it had a bedroom of its own, with curtains drawn to prevent drafts and a very light eiderdown plus a Shetland shawl ready for changes of temperature and humidity. I speak with authority here because I was more than once asked to "baby-sit" with that gamba when the Leo Smiths were away, warned to rush out first with the gamba in case of fire.

There were less direct educational activities. One of the most lasting in effect was his campaigning for music on academic curricula. Other musical leaders approved the principle, but Leo Smith was willing to trudge over and over again with the special committee of the Association of Women Teachers of the Toronto Conservatory (who spear-headed the active campaign), to present briefs and deputations in official quarters from Queen's Park to the City Hall.

He was a member of one academic society which has always seemed as mild as milk but which more than once has carried as far as the House of Commons in Great Britain the question of academic standards. This is the Union of Graduates in Music Inc., the membership of which is limited to those who hold music degrees, regular or honorary, from universities in the United Kingdom. Since 1893 it has been keeping a sharp eye on any trafficking in doctorates, and on the giving of degrees by organizations that have no proper standing, as well as on the standards of recognized institutions. It has also furthered general recognition of music on university curricula, and under its sponsorship a conference of professors of music was held in Oxford in 1949. With the pleased co-operation of the Archbishop of Canterbury it even turned a polite but firm eye on the historic Lambeth degrees, urging that standards be watched very carefully. There is incidental interest for Canadians in the fact that it was after this scrutiny, and when every care was being taken to sift names for such honours, that the first Lambeth doctorate in music came to Canada, honouring Healey Willan.

Leo Smith's participation in the Toronto Musicians' Association, more colloquially known as the musicians' union, throws further light on his personality. It is the very efficient association office which gives us our first certain date for Leo Smith's entrance into Toronto musical circles. He was initiated into the union on November 6, 1910. It was not his way as a scholar merely to obey rules grudgingly while taking potshots at policies from outside. The man who was a professor, and a conservative with both a large and a small initial letter, worked with jazz men, theatre men, bandsmen, concert artists, and enjoyed the work despite its problems. The members elected him to the executive board from 1946 until illness forced his withdrawal during 1951, and in February of 1952 they honoured him by a life membership.

"We were very fond of him," Walter Murdoch, president of the TMA, commented. "He was mild, sensitive, but effective, and he had a real and abiding interest in the profession. He was listened to, not merely in executive sessions but in general meetings. When he became a newspaper critic he showed what I knew before from our meetings, that his fairness was above personal bias. A tremendous person. We held him in warm affection."

One of the accomplishments of the union was the organization of the Toronto Proms in 1934 as a co-operative project to keep symphonic music popular and to give employment to musicians during the depression. From the first, the University of Toronto made the Varsity Arena available at a nominal rate. The feeling spread that the Proms represented something beyond any single institution, clique, or class, which indeed they did, and this appealed to Leo Smith. They became friendly events of summer Thursday nights, with attendance running as high as 8,000; and while programmes varied in quality, even the poorest years have had some high points in new music presented or in performances.

Leo Smith was first 'cellist in the Proms from 1938, wrote the programme notes, and served for years on the Prom committee. The Canadian Broadcasting Corporation and, later, CBC's television made live broadcasts. With more employment for musicians in the 1950's, the problems of the Proms have had new inflections, but Leo Smith's membership for years forms an example of ground worked with the result not merely of reaping an immediate harvest but of leaving a larger section arable for those who follow. The Proms enormously extended the public for symphonic music during a time when population was fast increasing.

Over the years, too, the list of Leo Smith's compositions grew in length and importance. He figured, for instance, in a historic hour for Canadian composers in February of 1935. The British Broadcasting Corporation put on an all-Canadian programme which was transmitted three times at hours convenient for people in all parts of the Commonwealth. The composers represented were Ernest Mac-Millan, Leo Smith, Healey Willan, Hector Gratton. Their works were heard by many in the Antipodes and Africa as well as Europe. But by few in Canada. The Canadian Broadcasting Commission (predecessor of the Canadian Broadcasting Corporation) did not bother to relay this historic first to Canadian listeners. Probably this was one of those times when, harassed by the exigencies of their duties, executives make or fail to make decisions, then wake up in the night and think: "I hope nobody ever asks me why we did that." Therefore one may well close the door on that minor skeleton in the cupboard of the CBC, which has done much for Canadian music. But it is important for the history of Canadian artistic evolution to record that, two decades before the much-publicized New York concert of Canadian music, and the Paris broadcast of this year, these senior men had rated for the Canadian composer a round-the-world broadcast from the Old World.

In September of the same year, Leo Smith's Quartet in D was broadcast by BBC. In October, it was performed in London at the South Place Concerts by the New English String Quartet, whose players expressed themselves as delighted with it. By a coincidence, the name of another man who has since come to participate in Canadian music appears on the same programme. The day's leaflet contained an advance notice of a concert by the Boyd Neel String Orchestra.

As performer, Leo Smith appeared continually, both on recital engagements and in orchestras. He was the first 'cellist from 1923 in the New Symphony Orchestra under Luigi von Kunits and later in the reorganized Toronto Symphony Orchestra under Sir Ernest MacMillan. Chamber music was probably what he liked best. He had played with the Conservatory Trio (Blachford and Guerrero), and with others including Dr. H. A. Fricker; then in 1929 the Conservatory String Quartet was formed. It was this quartet which gave the first performance of the Quartet in D in 1932 when, as newspapers reported, a chamber music audience stood at the end and cheered for five minutes.

The Conservatory String Quartet continued to play for several years in various parts of Ontario, including the National Gallery in Ottawa. One evening of the quartet in the early thirties has remained in memory as a kind of turning point in audiences and sponsorships. The J. B. O'Brians had invited a company to a final rehearsal by the quartet. The company was no longer, in some ways, so homogeneous as such a drawing-room audience might have been some years before. There was Miss Mortimer Clark, straight of back and regal in pale blue satin with court gloves to the shoulder—the last time we saw long white gloves worn to a drawing-room rehearsal. There were others among us who, if asked to name a prominent ancestor, might, like Pooh-Bah, have had to content ourselves with mentioning the amoeba. Private opinion varied as much. But—there was still unanimous agreement as to what constituted not only social but intellectual decorum. Perhaps that was the zenith, rather than the twilight of one period in Toronto; the base had broadened, but divisions had not yet taken place. The J. B. O'Brians graced the zenith.

With the expansion of the 1930's, some divisions were inevitable, if for no reason other than that the establishment of wider musical services involved questions of policy; making ends meet financially was an ever-present agenda item. As such questions arose, Leo Smith amazed even some of his friends of the 1920's by his readiness to spring into action like a commando. But it was always primarily for principles rather than personalities, as proven by the fact that some temporary estrangements were from persons in his closest personal circle.

Yet the growing pains of the 1930's did accompany growth, albeit the final development as seen today may seem to bear little resemblance to what preceded it. One single episode may be recounted because it is so apt an illustration. This episode concerned the Vogt Society. The Toronto Conservatory, harassed by financial problems, decided it must do without Dr. Healey Willan as vice-principal, and appoint a man who would find the practical administration more congenial. A resounding set of protests went up, with most everybody in musical circles from students to the Press involved in the *mêlée*.

Then there occurred an extraordinary sequence of events. In 1936, the Conservatory Residence Alumnae Association, in protest against the Conservatory's action, got a Provincial charter for an organization which it proposed to call the Willan Society. At the request of Dr. Willan, however, the name was changed to the Vogt Society. It set itself to the work of providing recognition of Canadian composers. At first the Society seemed to be emulating the Three Tailors of Tooley Street who spoke as "We the people of England." But, when hundreds crowded the recitals of new music, it became apparent that these musical Tooley Streeters had indeed spoken for a wide community interested in seeing that the bases of Canadian music should be broadened, not narrowed down.

Leo Smith took an active part in the Vogt Society and was president for a term. The Society's problems are not our story here, but the sequence of events is sharply pertinent. By degrees, there arose a policy of featuring younger composers or those less well known. The Society changed its name to The Society for Contemporary Music, and it was under these auspices that works by younger men such as John Weinzweig and Harry Somers were first heard. This society wound up. But when the League of Canadian Composers was formed, it had an established precedent from which to work. The older guard had given musical liberalism a voice and had drawn spectacular attention to Canadian composers.

A united front on new music was not consistently maintained by composers, and Leo Smith began to take an independent stand. The reasons were partly musical, partly non-musical. Some new music stressed the harsher aspects of life in the machine age, and Leo Smith disliked this in any key, old or modern. He did not resent the coming of new forms of music as such. From his earliest to his last written commentaries there are sentences expressing gladness, relief, or interest that music was being freed from old, tight strictures. And his own compositions provide scholarly examples of some new musical idioms. But his critical writings reiterate his sharp disapproval of artistic dogmatism. The records from both Europe and America show that many felt the *avant-garde* tended to assume dogmatic attitudes such as formerly had marked the academicians. In an unpublished article, Leo Smith wrote: "Too often liberalism assumes a high moral tone, a self-conscious superiority not conducive to doubt, to the testing of the validity of opinions."

This was the brief period when there were social counterparts of these new intellectual shuffles, when to have one's shoulder jostled by the Best People in an overcrowded, fashionable lobby was expected, and when speaking voices had to be raised an octave to be heard. To all jostlings, loud voices, artistic hardness and dogmatism Leo Smith's attitude recalled the exquisite finality of one sentence written by Beatrix Potter in her classic, *The Tale of Benjamin Bunny*: "Mr. Bunny held no opinion at all of the cat."

For one reason and another it came about that Leo Smith began to produce recitals of his works under his own sponsorship. And it was by his own music, and his own assessing of values, that his career moved towards its climax.

3. *Performer and Listener*

This change was an evolution in Leo Smith's career, not a new direction. He became less fully absorbed in the academic duties of teacher, lecturer, examiner; and more involved in another form of cultural leadership which, though it did not lead to abandonment of the classroom, embraced a wider public.

Leo Smith became a one-man institution within the great institutions to which be belonged. He was not lonely, but he was singular; and there is evidence that both his academic community and the broader public were ready to accept his singularity, increasingly aware of its quality. Students, international *confrères*, and personal friends well knew that he and his work were not merely part of a trend or a category. The man who was a living link in the evolutionary growth of a young nation's culture stood out more clearly defined to a larger audience.

The 1940's produced some of the most spectacular gatherings to hear his music. There was, for example, the night when the back wall of Strachan Hall looked like a great Gothic reredos of carved figures to the roof as people from the United States as well as Canada stood on furniture piled on furniture to gain standing room. It was one of the programmes he put on in collaboration with Trinity College and the Earle Grey Shakespeare Festival.

The period included the presentation of his finest compositions, the trios and the quartet for mixed consorts of voices and instruments. Programmes record the names of several performers, including the Harvey Perrin Choir for which he wrote several numbers. But two individuals require special mention: Marjorie Stevens Brown, into whose hands he most gladly put a viol and who was an untiring cohort in all his projects; and Myrtle Bruce Brown, his choice for his songs. Without her he would not present anything for voices.

Sometimes the anxiety among his friends was distressing, for none of his music had been recorded and the best had not been published. In his gradually failing health, Leo Smith was perhaps too insistent on having definitive performances or recordings under his own supervision, and so time slipped. One can remind a man that a train leaves in an hour or that his taxi is waiting; but not that death is waiting.

The bulk of his finest compositions is not great, but its aristocracy is distinctive. There are people who consider his few most distinguished works as among the most beautiful ever heard. He composed for solo voice, for ensembles of instruments old and modern, for ensembles of voices and instruments, for chorus and for orchestra. Admirers vary in the order of precedence they would give these pieces, but there is general agreement that important items include: the trios, for voice, 'cello, and piano; the Street Cries Quartet, for two voices, 'cello and piano; the best songs; the String Quartet in D; and the Summer Idyll for orchestra.

There is no special point in textual analysis because Leo Smith was neither a harmonic system maker nor a system breaker. In brief, he was not a system. He worked with easy freedom on rules he understood well enough to break extensively, so that the results were peculiar and pertinent to himself only. And he wrote to give enjoyment rather than to leave milestones in a revolution. But, because this man was so individualistic in character, there is possible advantage in relaying his reactions.

In symphonic work, homotonal Leo Smith was anachronistic in the same way as some atonalists are—both demand studious rehearsal in a modern day when orchestral rehearsal is very expensive. Leo Smith once recalled humorously a story of a noted musician playing Schoenberg, deliberately leaving out the accidentals. To leave out accidentals on purpose can be a laughing matter; to leave out accidentals accidentally can be fatal to a work.

Leo Smith's dissonances shimmered like the glistening

whitecaps on waves, resolving, never violating the sense of harmonic peace, and themselves bearing sweet relationships. But their subtlety demands accuracy. He said that he never wrote a note for mere texture. Each note was a character, a little illumination tracing the form and the line. Barlines are there, but his rhythms did not admit their tyranny. They had the free but inevitable certainty of waves coming to shore.

Played that way, the Summer Idyll has not too many notes and, like his ensembles, need not be hurried. It should not be typed with Delius. After praising the beauty of Delius' work, Leo Smith commented on his inadequate punctuation and failure to use the caesura. And he once wrote that the indecisiveness of Delius' personality recalled the story of Lord Balfour at a great reception, stopping at the top of a magnificent double stairway and explaining: "The worst of this staircase is that there is absolutely no reason why one should go down one side rather than the other." Leo Smith was as decisive as he was delicate. The best performance of the Summer Idyll was probably that under Fritz Mahler at the Toronto Proms: Leo Smith himself was first 'cellist and there was no danger of the strategic 'cellos coming in wrong, as has happened.

With the songs, there is a somewhat different problem. The vocal line is almost always to be regarded as the composer's subjective contemplation through music; not merely an expression of, but a reflective comment on the poem. Whether in rhapsody, glee, or gravity, the melodic vocal line of the songs may be seen, as it were, as the non-objective or abstract element of the tonal picture in which words and accompaniment form the objective or representational element. John Beckwith graced his student days by brightly pointing out in a *Varsity* review that Leo Smith wrote songs as most people like to read poetry, ruminating, pausing to savour an idea, and that he had the structural scholarship to accomplish this without distortion of poem or music. That is what Leo Smith said he intended.

This leaves a good role for the accompanist. In the masterly song "The Donkey," the accompaniment, with irregular rhythm, recalls the tonal actuality of the little hoofs as the donkey carried the Christ over a stony path, and the sound once heard must forever haunt anyone on Palm Sunday. The vocal line is the composer's illumined concept of this tender wonder, that one of the ugliest of God's creatures served to carry Christ. In "The Heavenly Bay," to Swinburne's poem, the word "Introspectively" beside the vocal line would have conveyed what he said he sought better than does the word "Intimately," which he has written. Again the accompaniment rolls gently like the water, while the vocal line is intended to suggest contemplative wonder at the peaceful beauty.

Some singers have complained that his vocal line is not a grateful one for the voice. The composer did take for granted a wide range, but that is not uncommon with mezzos today. When Myrtle Bruce Brown sang his songs in closest collaboration with the composer, sometimes almost as one singing in a trance, or in a subjective rhapsody, a spell was put on listeners; and what more can singers wish? John Coates chose the Leo Smith songs repeatedly. Mme Gadski said she would be pleased to have a volume dedicated to her. Reinald Werrenrath picked "The Prison Song" as one of the Hundred Best Songs.

Leo Smith never heard exactly what he intended in his setting of "We are the Music Makers" for women's voices. It too often sounded sacerdotal. This could mean that he did not succeed in writing his intent into his music there, as the number was performed by numerous good groups including the Toronto Mendelssohn Choir, and the Harvey Perrin Choir which gave the most studious devotion to presenting a number of his works. But it would be interesting to hear it tried once again when a conductor might tell the girl singers to master the notes and their breath control —then sing to give the illusion of being left breathless and a little frightened after seeing an unexplained phenomenon. This experiment might come near catching the wonder which Leo Smith felt for all that was unexplained in intellectual humanism as well as in nature. He respected science and became mystical only so far as concerned the riddle of human emotions. At that point he had full capacity for wonder and, like Bertrand Russell, would not be guilty of "cosmic impiety."

The rare jewels are his pieces for broken trio or broken quartet of instruments and voice. Here considerations may be more directly musical. The listener is sometimes fooled by thinking for a moment that an antique, modal influence will dominate; but he must be on guard, for, almost imperceptibly, the music broadens to include the present day. As quiet music as ever was written, these works can be hypnotic.

In November 1934, Lawrence Mason of the *Toronto*

Globe spoke of the Quartet in D as "typical ultra-modern music." But in March of that same year, Raymond Mullens wrote in *Saturday Night*: "Now this will never do. Mr. Smith, you have dared to write a quartet packed full of haunting melody, bubbling over with spirit, humor and life, obviously written with consummate skill but with learning subordinated to the effect desired. Don't you know, you poor benighted Toronto musician, that a modern quartet must be owlishly mathematical and incomprehensibly complex if it is to receive homage from those who profess to understand music? They will listen to your music, be entranced by its beauty—and, ashamed of their lapse from critical righteousness, promptly damn it."

These reviews are not so contradictory as they sound and did not indicate merely that yesterday's good hat was today's old hat. They denoted the fact that this composer was contemporary, but not within a fixed trend or system. On that point, the compositional technique of the trios and the Street Cries is an autobiographical testament—the composer was of his day but not cut off from the body of thought which, through the ages, had changed the little brain of primordial man into the intellect with modern capacity for humanistic genius.

Throughout his career, Leo Smith had what publicists call " a good Press." In the last decade, reviewers became ardent. Three oddly assorted adjectives appeared repeatedly: scholarly, intoxicating, quiet.

The night the Street Cries were first performed in Hart House Theatre, I listened from the door, having had some practical duties to perform. As the ovation broke out at the end, I leaned against the lobby wall in the dark, temples cold with fear and urgency; and found myself facing a young listener who likewise stared into space for the answer we did not know how to give at all. Staves, notes, lines, words, can be written down; but how perpetuate the ineffable quality of concepts?

There was one man, Colin Sabiston, then a member of the editorial board and sometime music editor and critic of the *Globe and Mail,* who had not only felt intensely the rare quality of the music but had an idea how the essence of Leo Smith's humanism could be given wider public expression. He knew Leo Smith's ability to identify himself with the listener. And he knew that Leo Smith conceived musical education to be the development of judgment and taste founded on some form of personal experience, for which purpose no form of indoctrination by mass methods is effective. Could Leo Smith, then about to retire from his professorship in the University of Toronto, be induced to start a new career as journalist in his late sixties? Oakley Dalgleish, editor-in-chief of the *Globe and Mail,* subsequently invited Leo Smith to become music critic, and so procured for his paper, and Canada, two memorable years of criticism.

In September, 1950, Leo Smith moved from the ranks of players and producers into the rows of the listeners, as critic on their behalf. It was a fitting culmination, for he himself had written: "It must be remembered that the listener, not the player, is the ultimate assessor of values."

By a lifetime of thought on principles, he became one of the fairly rare exceptions to the rule that fine professional musicians seldom make the most satisfactory critics for journalism. The question of objectivity is easy to analyse: if a creative man has not personal convictions, he lacks integrity as a creator; if a critic works on the basis of personal taste, he lacks integrity as a critic. The best artists may reach the necessary point of objectivity only to fall short in perceiving that their duty as a daily reviewer differs from that of the studio critic or the musicologist discussing aesthetics for the profession. He too often writes how-to-do-it criticism, and this has two absurdities. Even if several hundred thousand readers wanted to sit in on a coach's music lesson (most of them not having heard the performance and hence not knowing what the coach was talking about), it still would be an economic joke to use millions of dollars' worth of equipment and tons of newsprint to tell one performer how to play a note. Virgil Thomson is an outstanding musician-critic who has clearly stated the point that the journalistic critic is not writing for the performer but for the readers. Leo Smith saw all these factors in successful reviewing.

He was ready to tackle the work, but as one who dreaded noise and rushing he was a trifle apprehensive whether he could give satisfaction in the seeming hurly-burly of a newspaper office. The first night he walked across the city room to turn in his copy, typewriters stopped as eyes followed this unlikely figure. He was assessed. Then, with one accord, the journalists who were sophisticated enough to be callous to pomp and pretention, showed they were also sophisticated enough to realize what kind of man had come among them. Their affectionate respect wrapped him round. He was bowed into elevators first, and given precedence stepping off. It can be recorded for these Toronto editors and reporters that one of the most sensitive persons in Canadian culture said he had never been happier. It gave zest to his will to work on joyously, even after he was weakening in his fatal illness. He was now the journalist in full swing, keeping the copy moving, with a friendly feeling for the great roar of the presses through which he shared his ideas with thousands.

He had long given signs of his capacity for thinking on behalf of the public. Commenting on a rather obvious Tchaikovsky climax, he had written: "But it always sounds better than it looks to the musician." When members of the profession berated the public for not attending concerts in larger numbers, he wrote: "I suppose communities often become a little tone-weary." A scholar but no intellectual snob, he embraced in his sympathy the learned musician and the office worker who, having saved two dollars from his pay envelope to buy a ticket, hoped to enjoy a night out. He was gentle with innocent ignorance. Of one amateur opera where all soloists were off pitch, he wrote: "For the amateur first appearing in public, intonation is a problem." But he could be cutting when he felt the occasion warranted. Commenting on a composer who had turned from writing Broadway music to composing a standard symphonic work, he wrote with measured indifference: "It is the work of a master craftsman."

One review and one incident may be set down to epitomize essential elements in Leo Smith's criticism. He had listened in Massey Hall to a work which he esteemed but some aspects of which gave him misery. It was Bartok's Concerto for Orchestra presented by the Toronto Symphony Orchestra. Leo Smith praised Sir Ernest MacMillan's conducting and then wrote (in time for a midnight deadline) this prime example of setting forth both sides of a case:

> *Its style is not unfamiliar to those who know something of his other works, and many of his technical devices are familiar enough. The structure, the problem of unity between the movements, the fugal imitations, the shimmering effects, the glissandoes, the underlining of a melody at an unchanging interval suggestive of a river bank with objects reflected in the water—these and others are familiar.*
>
> *But the melodic idiom, the harmony, the chain of musical reasonings, the complex texture, more often than not seem to defy our previous experience. . . . At times I was absorbed with the cleverness of it all. The surging waves of sound, the mysterious shadow tints, the changing rhythms, the curious drone-like chord supports appearing often to have no harmonic connection with what was going on above, yet sounding strangely satisfying, the unusual cadences, the bits of lovely color, particularly for the flute and clarinet.*
>
> *Against this, however, it must be admitted that the music is hard and adamant. Only for a few fleeting moments in the fourth movement does the composer yield a little to simpler euphony. And surely it is unnecessarily difficult. The violins, for instance, scale to dizzy altitudes. That twenty or more should execute some daring gyrations in such altitudes without some discrepancy in pitch seemed to me to be possible only by the Grace of God.*

The other incident touched on his sense of integrity. It concerned a performance by a fine musician whom Leo Smith esteemed but with whom he felt no particular personal affinity. A music patron phoned, attempting to ensure an adverse criticism. Leo Smith was horrified that anybody should try to sway opinion in the Press against a musician and by endeavouring to influence the sincerity of writer or editor. He trembled and his arm had to be taken. He seemed near collapse. Then once more he came back fighting—making his last rally on behalf of integrity towards a man with whom he had often battled.

Such criticism formed the climax of a career chiefly academic but so romantic in its exploits and in the last gallant going forth in old age that it calls to mind Tennyson's lines from "Ulysses":

> *The long day wanes; the slow moon climbs, the deep*
> *Moans round with many voices. Come, my friends,*
> *'Tis not too late to seek a newer world.*
> *Push off, and sitting well in order smite*
> *The sounding furrows; for my purpose holds*
> *To sail beyond the sunset, and the baths*
> *Of all the western stars, until I die.*

His voyage ended on April 18, 1952. St. Stephen's Church was crowded for his funeral service, which was taken by a man he dearly liked, Canon J. E. Ward.

In the course of his life Leo Smith extracted an efficient working principle from humanistic theory. As a composer he bridged the gap between the old orthodoxies and new idioms. As a teacher of theory and composition he showed a younger generation, intent on yet newer innovations, how to be consistent as creative experimentalists. As a scholar exploring cultural backgrounds and as an essayist he gave vivid reality to his concept of historical continuity. His whole method of life was devoted to enriching the values of Western civilization.

Works by Leo Smith

(Works in the various categories have been listed approximately in the order in which the composer liked his compositions. Pending final disposition, manuscripts are in the combined custody of Myrtle Bruce Brown, Marion Brown, and Pearl McCarthy.)

CHAMBER MUSIC

Quartet in D for Strings   MS 1932
Quartet for Two Singers, 'Cello and Piano: MS
    Old London Street Cries
Trios for Voice, 'Cello and Piano: MS
    The Passionate Shepherd
    Her Reply
    Spring's Welcome
    Little Peggy Ramsey
Viola da Gamba and Voices: MS
    Arrangements of several Shakespearean songs
    Original music for "By a Bank as I Lay" (poem by
       Henry VIII)
    Whoop, Do me no Harm!
Viols and Voices: MS
    Arrangements of thirteenth-century responsories
    Lullaby (melody by Byrd)
Viola da Gamba, Voice, and Harpsichord: MS
    Transcription of "Adieu My Heart's Desire (Wm. Cornysh,
       musician at court of Henry VIII)
Trio for Violin, 'Cello, Piano: MS
    A Border Ballad

Works by Leo Smith

Trio for Violin, 'Cello and Harp: MS
   A Celtic Trio
Two Sketches for String Quartet, on French-Canadian folk
   melodies: MS
   Dans Paris y a une Brune
   J'ai Cueille la Belle Rose
Three Sketches for String Quartet, on British folk
   melodies: MS
   The Farmer and his Wife
   The Maid of Mourne Shore
   Loch Lomond
Four Viols: MS
   Variations on "The Carman's Whistle"
Shakespearean music for two treble viols and viola da
   gamba; gamba and harpsichord; one viol, gamba,
   and harpsichord   MS

ORCHESTRA

A Summer Idyll   MS
Elegy for Small Orchestra   MS
An Ancient Song (Henry VIII)   MS
Divertissements in Waltz Time   MS
Occasion for Strings; commissioned by Forest Hill Com-
   munity Concerts   MS

VIOLONCELLO WITH PIANO

Sonata in E Minor   MS 1943
Four Pieces in an Old English Style   SCHMIDT 1946
Sarabande and Gavotte, arranged from J. S. Bach's Sixth
   Suite for Violoncello   SCHIRMER 1915
Au Clair de la Lune (melody attributed to Lully)   HARRIS 1935
Four Pieces from the *Book of Irish Country Songs*, edited by
   Herbert Hughes; dedications to Frank S. Watson, Carl
   Fuchs, Madeline Mills, Doris Chapman   PUB. PRIVATELY
Indian Lament   MS 1915
Arrangements of Elizabethan songs   MS 1951
Intermezzo   MS

PART SONGS

Men's Voices Unaccompanied: SCHIRMER 1914
  On Dante's Track (Swinburne)
  Night (Swinburne); dedicated to J. Bertram Cullen
  Beloved and Blest (Swinburne); dedicated to Lena Hayes
Women's Voices Unaccompanied:
  A Roundel is Wrought (Swinburne)   MS
  Fresh from the Dewy Hill (Wm. Blake); dedicated to
    Dorothy Allan Park   ALEXANDER AND CABLE 1929
  We are the Music Makers (O'Shaughnessy)
                         ALEXANDER AND CABLE 1930
  We are the Music Makers (O'Shaughnessy), with harp
    and 'cello accompaniment; for the Harvey Perrin Choir   MS
  Time Long Past (Shelley)   MS
  To Music (Herrick); for the Harvey Perrin Choir   MS
  Night Piece to Julia (Herrick); for the Harvey Perrin
    Choir   MS
  A Dream (O'Shaughnessy); for the Harvey Perrin Choir MS
Arrangements; commissioned by the Harvey Perrin Choir: MS
  We Three Kings
  Sumer is i-cumen-in
  Cornish May Song
  Down by the Sally Gardens
Music for the "Dedication of the Fireplace," book by Alan
  Sullivan; for the fireplace of the old Arts and Letters
  Club, Adelaide Street, Toronto
        PARTLY PRINTED IN *The Lamps*, JUNE 1912

SONGS

The Donkey (Chesterton)   MS
Prison Song (Wm. Morris)   SCHIRMER 1919
Mad Song (Wm. Blake)   MS
Hear the Voice of the Bard (Wm. Blake)   MS 1941
Earth Raised up her Head (Wm. Blake)   MS 1941
Fresh from the Dewy Hill (Wm. Blake)   MS
Indian Songs: MS
  Whose Brother am I? (coll. Barbeau)

51

Works by Leo Smith

That's Why She was Born (coll. Barbeau)
Woman's Riding Song (coll. Barbeau)
Three Songs: HARRIS 1930
   June Lyric (Duncan Campbell Scott); dedicated to
   Mrs. J. N. Shenstone
   Imogen's Wish (Duncan Campbell Scott); dedicated to
   Myrtle Bruce Brown
   At Sunset (Duncan Campbell Scott); dedicated to Myrtle
   Bruce Brown
Spring Night (Duncan Campbell Scott)   MS
When Twilight Walks (Duncan Campbell Scott)   MS
Echo (Duncan Campbell Scott)   MS
The Heavenly Bay (Swinburne)   MS
Sometimes Forget (Arnold Smith)   MS
Five Songs; dedicated to Mme Johanna Gadski:
                        PUB. PRIVATELY 1912
   The Wild Flower's Song (Blake)
   The Laughing Song (Blake)
   I Love the Jocund Dance (Blake)
   My Star (Browning)
   Cradle Song (Swinburne)
New accompaniments for "The Laughing Song" and
   "I Love the Jocund Dance"   MS
Four Songs: SCHIRMER 1914
   I Saw Thee on Thy Bridal Day (Poe)
   Oranges (Leigh Hunt)
   My Mother Sea (Swinburne)
   To Helen (Poe)
New accompaniment for "My Mother Sea"   MS
Ballad of Dreamland (Swinburne)   MS
Songs in *Twenty-one Folksongs of French Canada*:
                           HARRIS 1928
   Je n'ai pas d'amant
   La Plainte du Coureur des Bois
Paraphrase on a Welsh Melody   MS
King's Ballad (Henry VIII)   MS
To Couple is a Custom (Henry VIII)   MS
A Robin Hood Ballad (paraphrase on an old English
    fragment)   MS

As I Walked Forth (Elizabethan ballad)   MS 1946
Little Pretty Nightingale (old English song)   MS 1951
The Dressmakers (Millicent Payne)   MS
Songs composed before 1910:   MS
   The Sleeper (Poe)
   The Lake (Poe)
   Three Shadows (Rossetti)
   Song of the Past (Shelley); the melody appears again in
    "Elegy for Orchestra"
   Ariadne (Leigh Hunt)
To One in Paradise (Poe)   MS 1924

VIOLIN WITH PIANO ACCOMPANIMENT

Tambourin, French-Canadian fiddle tune (coll. Barbeau);
   dedicated to Harry Adaskin   HARRIS 1930
Trochaios, French-Canadian fiddle tune (coll. Barbeau)
                                                      HARRIS 1930

PIANOFORTE

Transcriptions and Arrangements   GORDON THOMPSON 1942
Three Pieces: HARRIS 1937
   The Song Sparrow
   From an Old Note Book
   Schumannesque
Four Poems: MS
   A Lament
   A Cradle Song
   The Orange Tree

PUBLICATIONS

Music of the 17th and 18th Centuries   DENT 1931
Musical Rudiments   BOSTON 1920
Elementary Part Writing   HARRIS
Articles in the *Globe and Mail*, the *Conservatory Quarterly*
   Review and other magazines

This book is printed in eleven-point Linotype Times Roman, on Spicer's Bouffant Alpha vergé. Typographic design by Antje Lingner, University of Toronto Press. Portrait drawing of Professor Leo Smith by Dora de Pedery Hunt, from a study made by the artist on the occasion of Professor Smith's last programme in the Music Room of Hart House, University of Toronto, October 30, 1949. Chapter decorations by Richard Brown

Lightning Source UK Ltd.
Milton Keynes UK
UKHW012358200722
406167UK00001B/311